BAKING DAYS

BAKING DAYS

ENID BARON

HCE PUBLICATIONS / RIVERRUN ARTS

Alice Lindsay Price
HCE Publications/riverrun arts
26 East 25th Street
Tulsa, Oklahoma 74114
USA

Front cover photograph by Morton Shapiro/ibid stock photo
Photograph of Enid Baron by Elliott Lyon
Design by Carol Haralson

ISBN: 0-9641148-0-1

for L. R. B., with my love

CONTENTS

I

II

III

Acknowledgments

Many thanks to Alice Lindsay Price editor, publisher and poet for reading and rereading these poems. Her comments and suggestions have been more than helpful. And thanks to Ann Weisman who assisted in editing these poems.

Thanks to Joseph Parisi, friend and editor of POETRY, for his generous help and advice about many of these poems.

Several residencies at the Ragdale Foundation in Lake Forest, Illinois, helped to make the collection possible, due to the generosity of Ragdale founder, Alice Ryerson Hayes, and the Ragdale staff.

To Joseph Zendell and the Evanston Arts Council, grantors of my studio and refuge at the Noyes Cultural Center, my gratitude.

Some of the poems published here first appeared in slightly different form in the follwing publications:
Ariel, California Quarterly, Chester A Jones Contest, The Critic, Crosscurrents, Midway Review, Mother Poet , Korone, Rhino, Sing Heavenly Muse!, Spoon River Quarterly, Willow Review, Wooster Review, Yet Another Small Magazine.

Glossary of Yiddish Terms

THE ZADDIK'S DAUGHTER

For Serella, born in Vilna gubernya (Postova, Lithuania), 1900

Zaddik of the chicken flickers,
chestless in his long beard, materializing
on the Sabbath just long enough to seed
his Sabbath Queen, queen of the teppels,
siren of soupmakers, braiding her life
away in challah dough.

From this unmanned shtetl ship came
an eldest daughter, uncelebrated by custom,
unconsecrated, unclaimed, a throwaway daughter,
weaned before her time, sour
as old milk.

THE SINNER

Scooping a pale green half moon of melon,
she guides the silver spoon as if she's always
dined on bone china, sipped from crystal.
Beneath the soft light of the chandelier,
she looks a little pensive, as if
she is thinking of some story
she has read.

But if they watched her carefully,
they'd see her spoon pause in mid air.
Her reflection is a prayer that they won't notice
the awkward consonants that cling to her, like brine,
despite the hours she spends saying *cheerful*
and *children* and *church*.

They don't suspect that from the hiding places
of her big dark eyes, she is watching
their every movement: which fork they use
for salad, how they hold their knives and
how their linen napkins stay put
on their laps.

She is sure that God has seen her
take the pat of butter, watched her
eat from the desecrated plate. He must know
she breaks the Law of Kashreth for the first time.
But the soft chambray of her borrowed dress
is a curtain she lets fall over
Poland's hard stones.

LEARNING ABOUT LIES

I pretend to nap
in a darkened room while I listen to the click
of dishes set to dry on a white ridged drainboard,
the shriek of someone's forgotten kettle,
and the violins of the theme song
from "Helen Trent".

Because I cannot yet tell
time, I creep out too soon, sidle
into the kitchen where my mother sits by
the radio, trying to believe that " a woman over
thirty-five can still find happiness". Startled,
she scans my eyes for bags, and sentences
me back to bed.

As I lie there, waiting to be released,
I watch the larger hand circle,
as if by magic,
the small.

My Mother Teaches about Apricots

Taut skin never could fool her.
Her fingertips detected fraud in
ruby-red tomatoes, burstingly purple plums.
From her, I learned alertness to the pale flesh
below the surface, the disappointment
lurking, unseen.

Although I longed for milk chocolate bunnies,
she taught me the tart bite of an apricot,
the rough skin that makes the tongue
attempt retreat. A child could never
be too tender, she said, to learn
the taste of grief.

BAKING DAYS

Fifty years and still I smell her,
vanilla, and a little yeasty like bread.
My palms still feel the touch of her, pressed
against her smooth, flattened breasts.
I even taste her, not the milk she took away
because I sucked too hard and she was tender,
but the gift she gave those afternoons
she reached into the deep glass bowl
of the Sunbeam and offered up
her finger, instead.

When I am older, I slouch
into the kitchen to find her melting squares
of bittersweet chocolate in the double boiler,
humming some old song under her breath.
When she sets the Mixmaster to "Cream Butter",
I watch the pale thin sticks lose their edges,
their texture change with the sugar she adds.
Last, the slick stream of chocolate,
dark swirls which vanish
in the blend.

ELIEZAR'S SON

Someone with such eyebrows
should have been called Saul, a slayer
of Philistines, but his father, Eliezar,
a hider from Cossacks, called him
Solomon instead.

Eyebrows like those
don't prepare you for failure.
Such black brows, you think of a king,
someone whose fish comes fresh from
the sea, not pickled in brine
from a barrel.

Still, in the Heder,
he was the king, his prayers
pierced the stale, dank air like clear notes
of music. This one I will shape,
thinks the Rabbi,
this Solomon,
this lily.

They called him Sol in America.
Under the drone of the dentist's drill
he drove to make a living, he sang
to the Holy of Holies but no one
ever heard but He.

SATURDAY MATINEE, 1945

I was nine that afternoon when Dachau
made the newsreels, its skeletons stacked
like boards or still walking in their bones.
I squeezed my eyes shut,
made earmuffs of my hands,
but I had seen
the little piles of kindling
who were children, the smallest like dolls
the way their arms and legs landed
in the carts.

It was dusk when the show was over
and the empty streets stretched out like
mourners' ribbons. I crossed them, one by one,
barely breathing until I saw the light in
our apartment, and my mother making supper.
Up the stairs, I flew
past the Rivkinds' where Rachel lived,
past the Cohen twins above her, up past
Ruthy Greenberg's and her baby brother, Jake's—
the last flight to my door,
hungry now, home.

THE NIGHT VISITORS

"Amahl and the Night Visitors"
Opera by Giancarlo Menotti

After freezing on two streetcars
and roasting on the bus, we arrive
on the West Side where all the aunts
and uncles live except for Uncle Dave
with the chicken business in Los Angeles,
and Aunt Bea who lives near the lake
in an apartment hotel with Uncle Jack,
who is always trying to make us laugh
by barking like a dog.

In Aunt Sylvia's apartment, the radiators bang
and the steam heat hisses like there are snakes
inside the coils, and all the burners on the stove
have pots simmering.
Uncle Izzy and Uncle Jack and Uncle Sam
are puffing on cigars, and when I start to sneeze,
Aunt Edith asks if I'm catching a cold, dahlink,
to which I reply no, although I am.
I catch one every Christmas.

Uncle Irving bought a television set this year
and all the kids sit on the floor in front of it.
I sit between my cousin Rosey, who's my age but
acts like she's older, and my little cousin,
Phyllis, who gets to be flower girl
at all the weddings, the only
one of us who is fair.

We don't have television.
My father says he's waiting for it to get better,
although the truth is he's crazy about Jack Benny
on the radio, and Fred Allen and Eddy Cantor,
and doesn't want to watch Milton Berle
on the Firestone Hour, with snow.
Also, he doesn't have the money.

The uncles are playing pinochle
while the aunts chatter in the kitchen,
everyone talking at once, when I hear the sweetest
sound I ever heard from a boy who looks around
my age, a boy who walks with a stick and has
this high, beautiful voice,
like an angel's.

I move in closer to the set, crowding Rosey.
The boy, Amahl, is going on a journey with three men
wearing crowns and robes. The black king's voice
sounds like the earth opening. Amahl's mother
is making him promise he'll take care of himself
like my mother did when I went to summer camp
for the first time.

When my cousins get up one by one
to go play Air Raid in the bedroom,
I stay with Amahl, following the star,
my heart swelling and swelling
until I can hardly breathe,
as they make their way
to Bethlehem.

When they get to the manger,
everyone starts singing, and a miracle occurs:
Amahl can walk! I wish I were there too,
with the donkey, and the baby they say
is God's son. I start to cry and my father
looks up from his cards and asks what's wrong.

Nothing, I tell him, because how can I tell him
about wishing God would just once speak to me
so I'd know He was really there, and if when
you die, you know what happens afterwards or
does the you you are just disappear?
And what happens to the animals?

When the aunts call us to come and eat,
my cousin Howard hides under the bed.
They heap our plates with potato knishes,
plump slices of kishke and tzimmes with carrots
and prunes. On the table are quart bottles of Nehi,
orange and strawberry and rootbeer and grape.

Afterwards, out comes Aunt Anna's mandel bread
and Aunt Jean's apple strudel and my grandmother's
honey-dipped teiglach. Best is the angel food cake
my mother brought, cradling it in her arms
while she waited in the freezing slush,
twelve eggs high, and luminous
with sweet whipped cream.

As I head toward the bedroom with my cousins,
my father catches my eye. Feeling better, he asks?

Better than what, I wonder?

A Child's Passover

When my cousin Jack opened the back door,
Elijah, the Prophet, was hopping up and down
on the wooden porch, blowing on his fingers.
"Yankel", he scolded, "What took you?
I thought I would freeze to death."
Then he rushed past Jack
into the kitchen.

In the dining room, I asked where Jack was.
"He's letting in Elijah", said my father winking
at my mother who, as usual, didn't wink back.
Just then, there was a little sputter of
the candles, and in the blue goblet
at the center of the table
the sweet wine ebbed.

D IGITALIS

Lemon colored stalks, stalwart as
the days were hot and shining, those days they
peddled Vitalis on the radio, the summer
my father gave up cigarettes, arriving
at Pine Point Lodge in Wisconsin,
smoking a pipe.

When he came into the card room,
with his arched brows and beveled cheekbones,
my mother looked up only a moment
from her hand.
All that weekend, I made him steer me
around the shallows, although by that time
I could swim, and when he swam out
to deeper water, I went with him,
clinging to his back.

He'd put the pipe away
by the end of summer. In his shirt pocket,
I spied the red and white pack of Luckies
he never seemed to be
without.

The following summer,
when he hugged me at Parents' Day at camp,
I kept my distance from that
small, hard package
at his breast.

ENCAMPMENT

The women carry waxpaper-covered pyrex,
tent-lidded roasting pans, aluminum-domed
cake plates. The husbands converge with
thermos jugs and wooden hampers they can
barely lift. We stagger with folded-up card tables.
Once landed, we snap out the legs.

Everyone eats greasy brisket on rye bread,
kosher pickles, banana cake heavy as lead.
Washing it all down with Old Colony, the uncles
light their cigars and deal out the hands.
The aunts lower themselves, groaning,
onto blankets. "No swimming for an hour!
You'll get cramps and drown! Don't go
barefoot! Lit cigarettes, broken glass!"
The hour up, they call, "Stay
in the shallow!"

I wade, step by step, on the sandy bottom
until my lips feel the tickle of waves.
I know my mother, on her blanket,
can't see me, or my father
playing Pinochle for
a nickel a point.

Pushing myself up off my toes,
I swim out in the icy water,
deeper and deeper,
until I flip myself over and see
how small they look on shore.

ENID BARON   23

DIVIDING THE BREAD

Always it is the same,
Rose pushing past the others,
her small quick hands skimming
the hunks of bread, grasping them.
Hawkeyed Nathan swoops, snatches
the biggest piece, runs out the door.
Giving half of hers to the baby, Malke
slumps against the wall to glare at
Rose, on the floor, hunting crumbs.

Like a pack of wolves surrounding
a campfire, Rachel thinks. As she
chews her bread slowly, she
imagines a white room high above
an ocean, a table set with
crystal, pink frosted cakes.

Years later, she sits on a balcony
in Florida, waiting for her children.
At the restaurant, she breaks
her roll in little pieces, passes
them to each one
to eat.

Russian Tea: Moscow, 1985

Julia is bringing platters
of toasted sandwiches. I sit on
the sofa next to Leonid, who offers me tea.
Alexey, seventeen, translates, his black brows
joined together as he struggles for exactly
the right word.

I eat the sandwiches while Mila
talks about the trial in Gorky where they threw
her out of the courtroom before she could see
her husband. Lev, whose wife
and son got out ten years ago,
is drinking vodka.

I want to ask Julia
where she found such delicious white bread.
I want to ask her how she toasts the cheese
and still keeps the bread from burning.
I want to tell her my mother
could do this too.

But everyone is talking about Ari
who got three years hard labor
for teaching Hebrew. Julia passes
the plate of cakes to me. "Mother wants
me to tell you it's authentic," Alexey says.
"Flour, chocolate, sugar. No butter.
And never eggs."

MY FATHER SPEAKS OF HERRINGS

I

I curl myself around him like a small, green vine.
"So Goldilocks rides off with the prince," he states,
"and when they get to the castle, there is a
whole barrel of herrings which they eat
to their hearts' content."

I never notice Momma getting out of bed
until I hear the icebox door slam.
"And when the hunter saves Red Riding Hood,"
he avows, "the bubbe brings out the herrings
and everyone eats to their hearts' content."

II

One summer, after weathering a storm
that caged us in a moldy cottage in Cape Cod,
my husband and I headed for the lobster pier and
three-pounders that swung at the lobsterman
with claws as big as boxing gloves.

Like crazed surgeons, we hammered and cracked,
wielding the sweet meat with our fingers,
beaming at each other with greasy faces.

Brine or butter, what does it matter?
It's the feeling that, for once,
you got enough.

II

ONCE

Hungry mouths
bit and pulled me,
tore me like beaks,
and I flowed rich and sweet.

The bleat of a lamb-child
made me surge, cream-thick,
nipples rubber hungry
for the lip clamp.

The tick tock time
soaked me like a bather,
stained me with splashes,
and I was sucked like honey.

I rose swollen
in the sun bright morning,
and the course of my life
ran clear.

FIGS AT FIFTY

A million seeds
burst inside my mouth
each a dream of a purple ovary
bending, bending, breaking
its stem,
thudding against
the soft ground.

Sweet chaos,
this grit I taste joyfully
remembering the fullness
of summer.

Scene on Harbert Beach

Fat cheeks quivering
like a merchant's with a prospect,
he sits square-shouldered on the keel
of an upturned boat, a fourteen-month-old
potentate guarded by his mother.

One hunchbacked pterodactyl stops to admire
this newly minted coin. "Had one like that once,"
he says. "Fell out a window. Maid left it open."
Then he straightens himself like a tie,
and walks on.

The child doesn't see
the sudden wedge between his mother's eyes,
he only feels her fingertips soft
upon his head, once,
and once again.

CHICKS

Brass buttoned
in your sailor coats
you ran across the lawn in search
of robins' eggs, rainbow eggs, each
yoke a golden nugget.

My blue-coated babies,
your faces were open as the crocuses
I was too busy to see, sewing
your buttons, closing all the loopholes
so you couldn't run away.

This Easter I take you out for
brunch. Over wine, you talk of lovers
in words so quick and bright I can't
catch them, and I'm trying,
reaching out and grabbing to fill my basket.

ANDREW'S DREAM OF THE GREATGRANDFATHERS

Curvebacked, they straighten themselves up
for him, brushing ghetto dust from
rusty gabardines. Yeheskal's yarmulka
falls off his head without his knowing.
"Are you an angel?" he asks.

The other one, Mendel, touches his fingertips
to his lips, presses them against the boy's cleft chin.
Doing a little dance, they circle him,
searching for signs
of themselves.

So many questions: on the kibbutz,
do you wake to the bleat of a ram's horn
coiled toward heaven? Does the sound
break into your morning dreams, setting
them inside the Temple?

Do the women of the Sharon Valley
still bend to the well? When you climbed
the scorched trail to Masada,
did you find a sip of water
at the top?

LEAVETAKING

Old men in frayed sombreros
huddle on dirty plastic chairs.
A woman sweeps the waiting-
room floor with a crude broom.
Tugging at the cowl of her sweater,
my daughter shivers. I spread
my hand over the top of her head.

Two buses pull in together. We rush
to the first one, but someone shouts
it's the other. There's no driver, until
suddenly a man, his face as hard
as death appears. When I ask if this
is the bus to Mexico City, he nods,
then slides behind the steering wheel.

As he backs up, my daughter is
standing next to him, showing her
ticket. I search the window for
a friendly face, but all of them are
empty. The brakes screech as
the driver makes the turn.

On my way back to the casita,
the streets are filled with school children,
their books in little knapsacks on their backs.
I walk quickly toward the bakery, wanting hot
coffee, fresh-baked *bolillos*. But when I arrive,
the bolt is drawn across the weathered blue door.

THIRD CHILD

Susannah, the one I only thought about,
smiles at me now in dreams. My moon,
my plump one, she'll never leave me like
the lean ones with their quick intelligent faces.

This morning, the boy leaned down and let
me kiss him before he boarded the bus to
the airport. Then he turned, and all I could
see was his wide-waled corduroy back.

The girl, who would be Susannah's sister,
is leaving also, filling my attic with chipped
lamps from thrift shops, wobbly tables,
boxes marked SEND.

Each night, I wait for Susannah's first tooth
to shatter my sleep. But night after
night, she leans her sweet cheek against mine,
filling my ear with flute sounds that never break.

THE ANGEL OF DEATH APPEARS AS CROW

At first, I think Michael
home from school, slamming his basketball.
Thunk, it goes. Thunk. Starting downstairs,
I halt on the landing. It's my house,
not Michael's. I think someone
trying to leave a notice.
Thunk, it goes.

Through the gathered curtain,
I see no messenger, no slip of paper, only
twenty panes of glass, their balanced symmetry
suddenly broken. Darkly, a shape looms,
crashes against the door, looms again, crashes.
Like a bell clapper gone crazy.

As if through a veil,
I glimpse the Moloch ha Movis
spread black wings, crossed eyes focused
on small ears of Indian corn suspended
from pale, papery husks. Head first,
it hurls itself. Thunk.

From my side of the glass, I pound the door madly.
The crow flies up into the maple and, for the moment,
stays. As I mount the stairs, I listen for
a thunk that doesn't come. But how long
can I keep the glass from shattering,
the bounty from the beak?

CHERNOBYL

I

I was bending next to Olga,
while she talked about the dress
her father was going to buy for her
in Kiev. Past row after row of cabbages
she talked. It was to be blue,
with small flowers and a sash.

II

Afterwards
I was sent to my uncle's
outside Moscow. Olga was on the train
next to mine. She looked across the space
between us, yet she didn't seem to know me.

I tried to raise the window,
but the lock was stuck, so I rubbed a clean spot
on the glass. "Where are they sending you?"
I called, moving my mouth slowly.
But Olga's train pulled away.

III

Aunt and Uncle retire early.
They have given me the sofa for a bed.
Mornings when the hall lift wakes me,
I pretend the motor is the sound of the combine
Father drove in summer.

Above our heads the crows cawed
louder than usual, I remember,
but no whistle blew.

KILLING BOXES

*"The war against Iraq is being divided into killing boxes. . .
Iraqi tanks, artillery positions and the other targets are
destroyed in one box. . . allied squadrons move on to another."*
The New York Times
February 13, 1991

I

In ancient Babylon they kept a cormorant at court
trained to dive for the monarch's favorite dish,
a small, plump fish with yellow markings,
a sweet-fleshed specimen to which the cormorant also
was partial, waiting patiently for certain choice
morsels which he plucked with great care from
the king's outstretched hand.

It was rumored that upon his master's death,
the cormorant refused all food until
a grandson of the king had it carried to the sea,
where it raised its wasted head and breathed its last.
The king's grandson ordered the royal woodcarver
to construct a coffin of fragrant sandalwood.
The bird was laid to rest at
Nebachadnezzar's feet.

I I

At the treatment center in Jubail,
in a banana box with a hole cut for its head,
a cormorant is slowly dying.
It was found washed up on shore by a Saudi boy,
a lover of sea birds, who had unearthed beneath
the sticky thatch the cormorant of his dreams.
From the hole in the banana box, the bird retracts
its slender neck from hunks of cod flown in frozen
from a New England fishery. The box trembles
and trembles.

I I I

Centuries later, some digger
hits a burial mound. It is thought that
the ocean must suddenly have receded, or that
a tidal wave must have occurred. The remains are
identified in a bird book from the age of fossil fuels.
Among them: the heron, the egret, the frigate bird,
the booby, the roseate spoonbill, all extinct now,
all legends. Of the Great Cormorant, the book says:
"A noble bird. A favorite of kings."

THE COLOR OF MOURNING

On the morning after Martin
met the death he dreaded and expected,
on a street where white folks were sprinkled
like refined sugar, I turned my headlights on
to show that I, too,
was in mourning.

Suddenly, a young man shot out
into the street and struck my window,
the flat of his hand like crushed rose petals
against the glass.

"Turn your goddam lights off, honky!" he screamed.
Swiftly, I did, and as if with his eyes,
saw the lights dim, the blank,
empty lens, the void.

FAMILIES

At Amboseli,
we spotted a chain of elephants,
traveling like a freight train
across the savannah.

But trouble came,
as trouble comes to all creatures,
when one of the young ones
plunged into a water hole.

Halting, they surrounded
the clumsy calf in his muddy bath,
reaching out their ropy trunks to him,
trumpeting to him to take hold.

From the Land Rover, we watched
as the clan tugged and shoved
the little elephant
from the ooze.

No one scolded. Instead, they grazed him
with the velvety tips of their trunks,
as if to comfort him, and perhaps
to comfort themselves.

When they picked up steam again
and filed past, I recognized his mother.
She was the one he lumbered along with,
his ears flapping like flags.

When I was eight, I would lie awake nights,
trying to pick which of my five aunts
I would live with, if anything
should ever happen
to my mother.

Those were the days when humans
were like elephants.

Those lucky days.

PRIMIPARA

We clung the only way we could
those days. Spoonwise. You the stem,
and I the big round bowl.

Our movements were gentle,
reverent, rocking her,
we said.

Your ear against my belly,
you drummed softly, vowed
she answered back.

~

On a chill November day,
you drove me to the hospital
along a lake of molten lead.

In the playgrounds,
all the swings were still,
like gypsy moths in early morning.

Under my red coat, she rode, frozen,
as if she sensed our life together —
about to end.

THE PACT

This is the way they arrange it:
she feigning sleep, he feigning
he believes her, trying not
to stir the common sheet
resting on her silent back.

The sign that he sleeps
is a whistle, slow and steady
as a clock. Hers might be the sound
of glass against granite. (He would not
know how to tell her if she asked.)

This is the way they have always
arranged it, he the dreamer, she
the keeper of dreams, clinging
to her side of the mattress,
its hard, reliable edge.

EVENSONG

He stands at the kitchen door,
looking in at her through the glass.
He is hoping she'll step away
from the red saucepan, lay down
her spoon or ladle, and walk towards him.

Sometimes when she doesn't hear
his footsteps, she looks up to see
his glasses shining outside the door.
Even on freezing winter nights,
when his cheeks are as red as the sauce-
pan, he waits for her to cross the kitchen
and let him in.

But for her,
it is like praying
the same words over and over,
when what she wants
is something beautiful to say

When she doesn't open the door for him,
she is searching for something beautiful
to say.

AT THE KIRIN OFFICE: TOKYO

"Dozo, Dozo*," I say, bowing,
the glazed cup burning my fingers.
Cloudy gray with brown markings,
three times I have dropped it.
Mr. Yamato smiles politely
each time I tell him.

I write home to Chicago:
"Japanese men get drunk
after work, and crowd into trains.
Japanese women are used
only to xerox and serve tea.
Japanese cups have no handles."

My mother writes back:
"In middle age, your greatgrandmother
got too fat to walk on her tiny feet,
requiring transport from room to room.
Her husband named her Old Wife Who Is Useless."

Today I refuse to serve Mr. Yamato.
"You take it," I tell Miss Tamei.
"You burn yourself. Not me."
When she returns, she murmurs,
"Yamato sad not to see you."

After work, at the tea shop,
I buy a blue cup with three white cranes.
On the train, the man standing in front of me
swivels his head to see the small sharp box
I hold against his back.

[*Dozo means thank you.]

MASKS

The sand gives way as we walk,
and we keep sinking, as if each of us
has one short leg. After twenty-five years,
Joan still smears suntan oil over
Frank's fishbelly white back.
As we limp along, she says
she was once in love
with a married man.

Trying to concentrate on not stumbling,
I say,"The sand seems to be
more solid farther out."

Just then, the two men turn around,
the one so frail he seems transparent,
the other, bearshaped, his round flat face
like one of those reticulated masks
which, opened, reveals
another face beneath.

JOCOTES

We had seen them in vendors' carts
in San Jose, small green fruits like unripe
tomatoes but less round. Here, in Guanacaste,
they lie scattered at our feet as we sit
in rapt attention to the huge red ball
hovering at the edge
of a darkening ocean..

When the sky has lost its luster,
we fill our hands with all the ripe ones
and cart them back to our room.
From our balcony we watch
the constellations appear,
shyly at first, then boldly.
Like children, I think.

After dinner, after the short walk
on the sand, the waves crashing against the black
rocks, when the chicharras begin
their racket in the trees, we eat
the fruit slowly, sucking on the pits
when the flesh is gone.

MONTEVERDE

On the way down the mountain,
Mañuel stops the Jeep
to get us marinones while we wait,
sweating on the vinyl seats,
the only sound Mañuel beating
branches with a stick, fruit falling,
heavy, on the ground.

When he climbs back in the Jeep,
he is smiling, his hands filled with
fat red fruits bearded with cashews
in shells we can not break.
The juice from the bright orange meat
drips down our chins, filling
the Jeep with the smell
of cashew fruit.

Mañuel is quiet after that, his eyes always
on the road. The boulders are very big,
and there are no guard rails.
I lick juice from my fingers and
palms, and sometimes, when he shifts gears,
his hand brushes my bare thigh.

My daughter curls up
in the back seat but it's too short
for her, and her legs stick up
like stalks behind our heads
all the way back to town.

SEDUCTION AT THE VILLA DEL SOL

Simones, the one-armed birdman,
makes his way across the sand to where we
are outstretched on our lounges, turning
slowly on yellow towels, basting
in coconut oil, barbecue for
the bright painted beaks of his birds.

He squats in front of us and reaches
with his one hand into the sack beside him.
Out comes a yellow toucan with a brilliant
orange beak. Ann is sitting up now.
Next is a lapiz splashed with crimson
and white. Susan, kneeling next to him,
asks the price.

Although I feel my flesh burning,
I don't turn away. The arm that isn't
there holds me, the hand that can't
use the paintbrush keeps me there.

By mid-morning, Simones is far away,
his empty sack flapping against his back,
the lapiz bird next to my lounge,
a beacon to all the basket girls,
bead sellers, dress vendors, who shoeless,
will trek the hot sand all morning.
Simones has made the way.

AT PETRODVORETS

Nicholas leans gingerly against Venus,
having been burned once by a golden breast.
"Sunny," he calls to the Czarina.
"How much longer must I wait?"
In the servants' wing, Masha applies wax
for the last time to her floors.

"I was only the wife of the gardener,"
Masha testifies to the court. Twenty years later,
she is incinerated in an air raid in Leningrad.
When the architect, Lobovikov, is sent for
after the war, he is assigned Masha's
apartment. The peasants

grumble about leaving. Their poultry
roost on Masha's floors. After Lobovikov
starts restoring the palace, his wife,
Ina Rozhanskya, begs for a little wax.
"Just a jot," she pleads, "to bring back
the color." But all the wax is allotted

to the palace where tourists don
felt slippers at the door. From such
buffing, the patina comes back
once more.

AT THE CHARLES DARWIN RESEARCH STATION

It is a child's face,
an ancient's, all eyes,
the neck a withered stalk aimed at the Keeper,
who calls: *Ven, Luís.*
Ven, mi querido.

Knock-kneed, Luís lumbers, his scaled legs,
armor against the scorched ground,
his shell a saddle, a dark map of a
hard land he will never see, a terrain
he will never ride on.

Air whooshes in and out of his pinprick nostrils,
in and out, in and out, the sound
of passion. Some would say
the sound of love.

Bending to plant a kiss,
the Keeper bids Luís to hold his head out
for the cameras. "Twenty years,"
he tells us.
"We two."

~

With the old-fashioned camera you refuse
to replace, you are down on one knee.
But who is kept, and who keeper?
We, thirty-two.

The Courtship of the Blue-footed Booby
(Sula nebouxii)

A tramp without a derby,
he does a two-step around his lady,
elbows flapping, bill and tail sky-pointing
to what a high flyer he is
once his flat feet leave
the ground. She,

the hub of his wheeling,
bull's eye of his feathered arrow,
stands immersed in turquoise,
her button eyes unblinking. He
raises his azure platters,
lays them down at her feet.

"Whew!" he seems to whistle,
wanting her to adore him.
"Awk", she squawks.
What she wants to know is
how good is his diving,
how accurate,
how deep.

BLUEGRASS FESTIVAL

Bill Monroe was singing "I'm Travelin' On and On",
but when the rain began, we fled
as we would not have done for
Itzhak or Yehudi or Yo-Yo,
you leading me by the hand down
the straw-strewn aisle between
the tarps blanketing the ground,
dense colonies of true-bluegrass disciples,
fathomless to night-blind me.

Recalling "trustwalks" of the 70s,
those years we almost broke apart,
I stumbled along behind you,
my shining sneakers my only marker
against the ground, yours, that distant light
growing closer and closer, until even I
could see we were almost home.